READ ABOUT

Earthquakes

Anna Claybourne

COPPER BEECH BOOKS
BROOKFIELD • CONNECTICUT

Contents

© Aladdin Books Ltd 2000

Designed and produced by
Aladdin Books Ltd
28 Percy Street
London W1P 0LD

First published in
the United States in 2000 by
Copper Beech Books,
an imprint of
The Millbrook Press
2 Old New Milford Road
Brookfield, Connecticut 06804

ISBN 0 7613 1172 6
Cataloging-in-Publication data is on file
at the Library of Congress.

Printed in Belgium

All rights reserved

Editor
Jim Pipe

Science Consultant
Dr. David Pyle

Series Literacy Consultant
Wendy Cobb

Design
Flick Killerby Book Design and Graphics

Picture Research
Brooks Krikler Research

Earthquake!

Being in an earthquake is very scary. First people feel the ground starting to move. The walls shake and rumble. Pictures fall off their hooks and books fall off their shelves. And that's just a little earthquake!

In a big earthquake, the ground jerks up and down like a fairground ride. Walls collapse and houses fall apart. What should people do if they are in a big earthquake?

These people are looking at their home. It collapsed in an earthquake.

Earthquakes can start fires. How? Answer on page 32.

They could stay inside. But what if their house fell down and they got trapped underneath? They could run outside, but would they be safe?

In an earthquake, trees and lampposts fall over, and bridges collapse. Big cracks open up in the ground. It's not safe anywhere! Earthquakes only last a few minutes. But even when the shaking stops, there is still danger.

Earthquakes destroy roads and railroads. But a helicopter can still rescue some people.

People become trapped under collapsed buildings, burst pipes squirt water over everything, electric cables snap. Roads crack and become blocked by fallen trees.

In a big earthquake, thousands of people can lose their homes. In a cold winter, it is hard to find a warm place for them to live in.

After a large earthquake in Turkey, hundreds of people had to live in these tents.

Do you want to know more about earthquakes? Read on and find out all about them, why they happen, and how to stay safe in them.

Under the Ground

Why the Ground Moves • How Earthquakes Start

The San Andreas Fault in California. Here two plates have met and caused a split in the earth's crust.

You don't feel it, but the ground is moving all the time.

The surface of the earth is made up of rocks that are always changing and moving around.

For example, Africa and South America are moving away from each other.

They are moving very, very slowly — only about as fast as your fingernails grow.

The surface moves so slowly that usually no one can feel it. But sometimes the ground jumps and jerks in big, sudden movements. That's what an earthquake is.

To see why this happens, you have to look at the whole earth. The earth's surface (the outside part we live on) is called the crust.

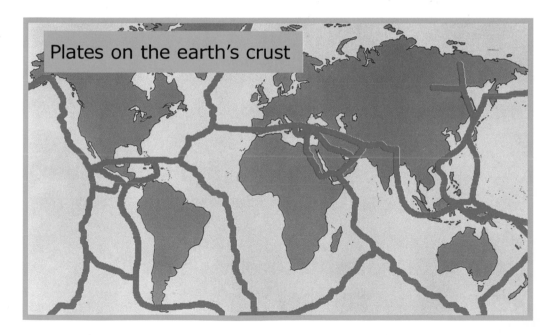

Plates on the earth's crust

The crust is made up of big pieces of rock, called plates. One plate can be thousands of miles wide. Look at the world map, above.

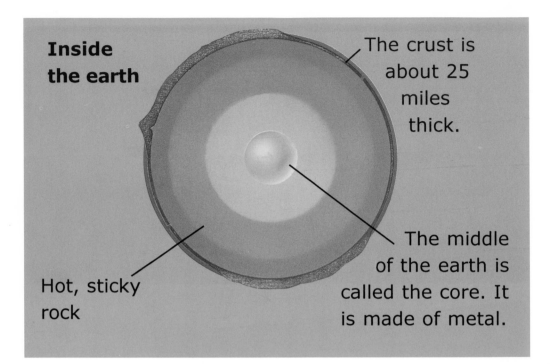

Inside the earth

The crust is about 25 miles thick.

Hot, sticky rock

The middle of the earth is called the core. It is made of metal.

Inside, the earth is full of hot, sticky rock. At the surface the rock melts. The plates float on top of this melted rock, which is called magma.

The earth's plates fit together a bit like a jigsaw puzzle. But they don't fit exactly. They're not quite the right shape.

You can't see the edges of most plates. They're covered up with soil, grass, or buildings.

Sometimes hot magma pushes up in a weak point between the plates. This can cause a small earthquake.

The plate edges may also overlap or get squashed together. They push against each other with a very large force — and that's how big earthquakes happen.

Magma can cause an earthquake when it pushes up at weak spots in the earth's crust.

Edges of two plates

Magma pushes upward and pushes plates apart.

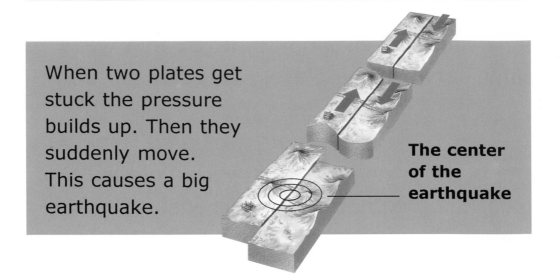

When two plates get stuck the pressure builds up. Then they suddenly move. This causes a big earthquake.

The center of the earthquake

The worst earthquakes happen when two plates scrape against each other and get stuck. Each plate is pressing against the other but they don't move. The pressure builds up and up.

Then, one day, the plates suddenly slip. The earth jolts and jumps in a massive earthquake.

Big earthquakes can make the largest buildings fall down.

Earthquake Zones

Where Earthquakes Are • Under the Sea

Most earthquakes happen at the edges of the plates. These places are called earthquake zones. So, where are the earthquake zones? This map of the world shows the main ones. The lines show the edges of the plates.

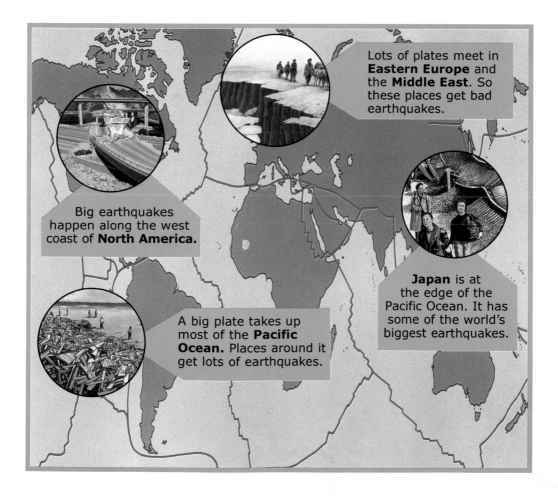

Lots of plates meet in **Eastern Europe** and the **Middle East**. So these places get bad earthquakes.

Big earthquakes happen along the west coast of **North America.**

Japan is at the edge of the Pacific Ocean. It has some of the world's biggest earthquakes.

A big plate takes up most of the **Pacific Ocean.** Places around it get lots of earthquakes.

Some earthquake zones are under the sea. When there's an underwater earthquake, there are no buildings to fall down and no one gets squashed. But underwater earthquakes aren't safe. This is what happens...

An underwater earthquake is just like an earthquake on land. The seabed jolts and makes the water on top move as well.

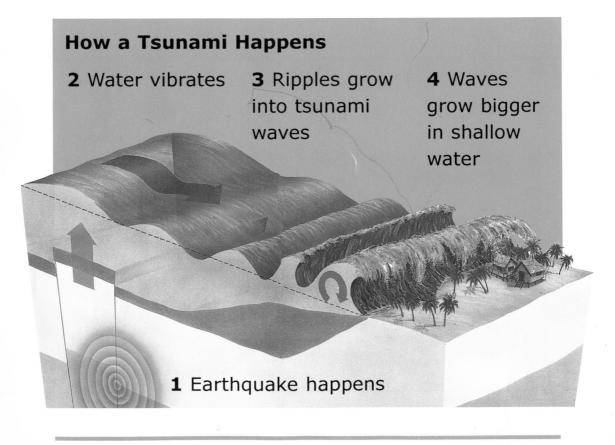

How a Tsunami Happens

2 Water vibrates

3 Ripples grow into tsunami waves

4 Waves grow bigger in shallow water

1 Earthquake happens

What has happened? Answer on page 32.

The sea water starts to shake and vibrate. The vibrations get bigger and bigger until they turn into a very big, very fast wave called a tsunami (say "sue-nah-me").

The wave moves very fast, growing taller and taller as it gets closer to the land. When it crashes onto the shore, a tsunami can be 150 feet tall.

Tsunamis can flatten seaside towns. So they can be as bad as an earthquake on land.

Earthquake Danger

Big and Small Earthquakes • Damage

Earthquakes can be tiny — or very, very big.
Little earthquakes are called earth tremors.
They're so small, you might not feel them at all.

But the biggest earthquakes flatten cities and
kill thousands of people.

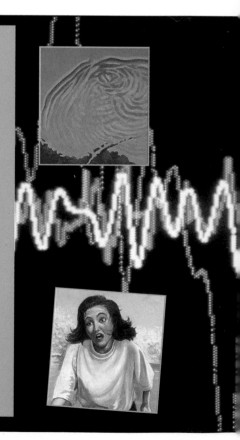

The Richter scale measures
earthquakes from 1 to 10.

1 You can't feel an
earthquake this small.

2 Scientists spot these mini-
quakes, but you wouldn't.

3 What was that? You might
notice a little rumble.

4 At 4 on the scale, you can
feel the ground shake.

5 At number 5, things are
getting scary.

Scientists use the Richter scale to measure how big an earthquake is. The Richter scale was invented nearly 70 years ago, by a scientist named Doctor Charles Richter.

Some earthquakes are between numbers. For example, 8.4 or 8.5 on the Richter scale means an earthquake in between 8 and 9.

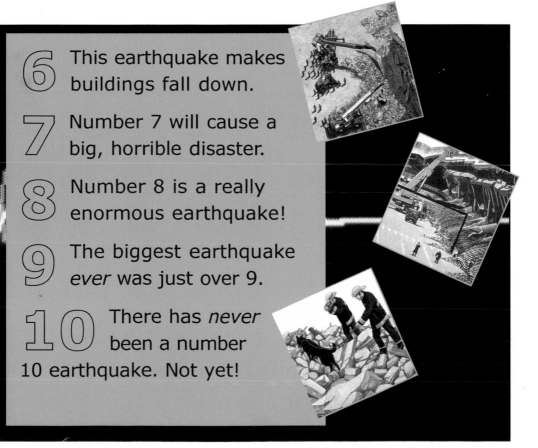

6 This earthquake makes buildings fall down.

7 Number 7 will cause a big, horrible disaster.

8 Number 8 is a really enormous earthquake!

9 The biggest earthquake *ever* was just over 9.

10 There has *never* been a number 10 earthquake. Not yet!

Which are the most deadly earthquakes? It depends on where they happen. The worst earthquakes hit crowded cities.

The biggest earthquake ever was in Alaska, about 35 years ago. It scored 9.2 on the Richter scale, so it must have been very shaky and very frightening.

Only a few towns in Alaska were hit by the big earthquake.

But Alaska is a very empty place. Not many people live there. Only 131 people died in that earthquake. If it had been in a big city, many more people would have been killed.

Earthquakes force many people to move home.

In 1985 another earthquake hit Mexico. It was smaller than the Alaska earthquake. But more than 10,000 people died, and many more lost their homes.

A big hospital fell down and many of the doctors and nurses died. Lots of injured people had nowhere to go.

Why was it so bad? Because the earthquake hit Mexico City — one of the biggest, most crowded cities in the world.

A long time after the shaking stops an earthquake can be dangerous. People may be stuck under the rubble.

Earthquakes also damage roads and bridges. Sometimes helicopters are used to help people quickly.

There may be no clean water, nowhere to buy food, and nowhere to get medicine if you are ill. There can be many extra earthquakes, called aftershocks, after the main one.

When buildings fall down, people often get stuck under the rubble.

After a big earthquake, people travel from all over the world to help rescue the victims. Some countries send rescue teams to dig people out of the rubble.

Firefighters put out a fire started by an earthquake.

The teams often have dogs that are trained to hunt for people in the rubble. The rescue teams also bring tents for people to live in. They give them food, water, medicine, and blankets.

As well as people, some countries send money. It is used to help the earthquake victims rebuild their towns. Houses have to be built again, and roads and bridges must be repaired.

Doctors have to work in the ruins.

This baby is being pulled from the rubble.

Earthquake Science

Even scientists can't tell people what hour an earthquake will strike. But they try to warn us.

There are often a lot of earth tremors (mini-earthquakes) before a big earthquake. They are a warning sign. If there is time, people can leave the area before the earthquake hits.

So scientists look out for earth tremors. They use a machine called a seismometer (say "size-mom-it-er"). A seismometer can feel the ground moving.

A creepometer is an underground machine that measures how much the earth's plates are moving.

A seismometer can spot movements that are too small for us to feel.

The seismometer is attached to a pen that draws a line on a roll of paper. The zigzags show how much the ground is shaking. A big zigzag shows an earthquake.

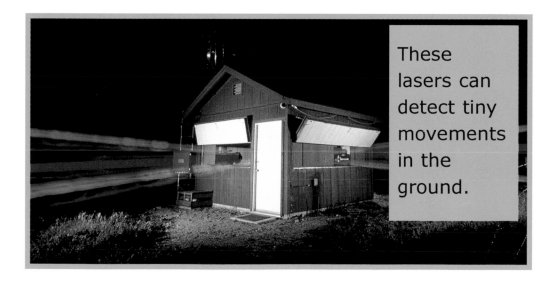

These lasers can detect tiny movements in the ground.

Scientists also use lasers to see if the earth is moving. The laser shines a very narrow beam of light. Even a tiny movement in the ground makes the laser beam shake.

Even thousands of years ago, people knew that earth tremors could mean an earthquake was coming.

A Chinese scientist named Chang Heng wanted to warn about earthquakes nearly 2,000 years ago. He invented an early type of seismometer. It looked like a large jar.

China has a history of deadly earthquakes. One that hit Shansi 450 years ago killed 830,000 people.

On the outside of Chang's jar were parts that looked like dragons. Each dragon held a ball in its mouth.

If there was an earth tremor, the dragons' mouths opened. If lots of balls fell, it warned of a big earthquake.

Staying Safe

What if a big earthquake happens?
Well, many earthquake zones have special
buildings that won't fall down, even in a
large earthquake. These are called
quake-proof buildings.

Long ago, many houses in Japan were made with light, paper walls.
Why would paper walls be good in an earthquake? Answer on page 32.

Modern quake-proof buildings have strong, flexible, steel frames.

They bend and wave around instead of breaking. After the earthquake, they're still standing.

When a big earthquake hit Kobe, Japan, lots of new buildings were still standing. They were built to resist earthquakes.

This quake-proof skyscraper is in San Francisco, California. This city has often been hit by earthquakes.

When the earthquake hit Kobe in 1995, many old buildings collapsed.

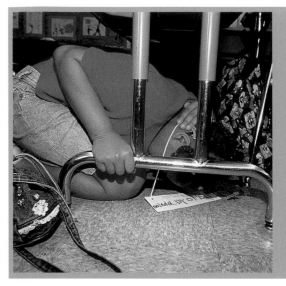

The safest place in an earthquake is under a big table or desk.

If you are outside when an earthquake strikes, run away from trees and buildings.

But what if people are not in a quake-proof building? Earthquake scientists say the best thing to do is to hide under a strong table, and hold on tight to one of the legs.

People shouldn't go outside, because something might fall on them from high up.

Nobody knows where the next earthquake will hit, or how big it will be. But in some earthquake zones, like California and Japan, everyone is ready for a big earthquake.

People here have special kits containing food, medicines, and blankets to help them survive if the earthquake destroys their house.

Don't worry — there are only a few big earthquakes every year. With luck, you won't ever be in one. But if you are, at least now you know what to do!

These cars are part of an earthquake safety drill in China.

Find Out More

PICTURE QUIZ

Can you think of five things that happen in an earthquake? Look at the pictures below for some clues. They can all be found in this book. The answers are on page 32.

UNUSUAL WORDS

Here we explain some words you may have read in this book.

Aftershock A small earthquake that sometimes happens after a big one.

Core The center of the earth.

Crust The hard layer of rock around the earth.

Focus The middle of an earthquake, where the shaking is strongest.

Focus

Laser A machine that makes a narrow beam of light.

Magma Hot, sticky, melted rock inside the earth.

Plates The huge pieces of rock that make up the earth's surface.

Quake-proof Quake-proof buildings are built so that they stay standing in an earthquake.

Richter scale A scale of 1 to 10, used to measure earthquakes.

Rubble All the parts of a building that has just fallen down, like bricks and dust.

Seismometer (size-mom-it-er) A machine that spots movements in the ground.

Seismologist (size-moll-oh-jist) A scientist who studies earthquakes.

Tremor or **earth tremor** A very small earthquake.

Tsunami (sue-nah-me) A giant wave caused by an earthquake.

Vibrate When something vibrates, it shakes very fast.

Earthquake Myths

Many ancient peoples thought that earthquakes were caused by monsters. In Indian myth, the world sits on eight elephants. When an elephant shakes its head, there is an earthquake.

EARTHQUAKE DISASTERS

San Francisco 1909

This earthquake lasted for 40 seconds, but it was very strong. Over 28,000 buildings were ruined, and 250,000 people lost their homes.

Yungay, Peru 1970

An earthquake shook ice off the top of the Andes Mountains. The ice turned into mud and swept away the town of Yungay. 50,000 people were killed.

Before   After

Yalova, Turkey 1999

Sometimes big earthquakes happen one after the other in the same area. Turkey was hit by many large earthquakes in 1999.

Index

ANSWERS TO PICTURE QUESTIONS

Page 4 Earthquakes start fires if they happen when people are cooking. They make stoves and hot pans fall on the floor.
Page 13 A tsunami has swept these boats from one side of the wall to the other.

Page 25 Paper walls hurt less if they collapse in an earthquake.
Page 30 In an earthquake trees and buildings fall down, fires start, the ground shakes, roads are cracked, pipes burst, people are trapped, tsunamis happen.

Illustrators: Pete Roberts, Graham Green – Allied Artists; Mike Saunders, Gerald Wood
Photocredits: *Abbreviations: t-top, m-middle, b-bottom, r-right, l-left, c-center.* Cover and Pages 3b, 4, 6 &19 – Rex Features; 1, 18b & 27 – Eye Ubiquitous; 5, 10, 13, 14-15, 18t, 20, 21, 23, 28 & 29 – Frank Spooner Pictures.